Big Stories for Little Children

A "Grampa Bill's" Farm and
Animal Story Collection

Bill Wilson

AuthorHouse™ LLC
1663 Liberty Drive
Bloomington, IN 47403
www.authorhouse.com
Phone: 1-800-839-8640

Published by AuthorHouse 06/24/2014

ISBN: 978-1-4969-1270-1 (sc)
        978-1-4969-1271-8 (e)

Library of Congress Control Number: 2014909059

authorHOUSE®

I dedicate this book to the inquisitive and wondrous minds of little children, in that they may know and appreciate the wonderful world of animals and nature.

I also dedicate this book to my grandsons, Aiden, Ian & Liam Wilson, may you always live life seeking God's wonder.

One Sunny Day

Bright white clouds were scootin' across a beautiful blue sky, bumping into each other and allowing a bright golden shaft of sunlight to brighten up Grampa Bill's farmland, called "A Touch of Nature" as he and Gramma Sue had named it. As he stood there, his thumbs hooked in his brand new red suspenders, admiring Gods beauty, a scripture from the bible came to mind. "This is the day the Lord has made, let us rejoice and be glad in it." Yes, he was glad. At the far end of his back yard, Daisy a one year old doe, (a doe is a girl deer) was sniffing the chickens in their outside run. The chickens were all in a bunch, eagerly trying to get a look at this new creature! Bertha, our chicken in charge, (C.I.C.) gave Daisy a peck on the nose! Daisy jumped back, surprised but not hurt. Grampa Bill said," That was just a kiss, Daisy." Daisy trotted back to the garden and laid down among the peppers and tomatoes. She said, "I'm having a time getting used to all these new animals, I never saw anything like that in the woods by the creek where I was raised."

Grampa Said, "Each Sunday after church I usually take a walk around the farm, if you'd like, I'll introduce you to all the animals in my Farm Sanctuary." Daisy said, "that sounds great, I'm looking forward to that."

Willie the wren, who lived in one of Grampa's bird houses flew down to Grampa's shoulder. "Nice suspenders, Gramps, who is that big brown and grey animal in the garden?" "Oh, that's Daisy, she's a young deer, a doe, that means she's a girl deer, a new addition to our farm." "She's pretty big for a girl," Willie said and flew away, "gotta feed my children."

Grampa walked over to the corral where Howard was standing, he liked to rest his chin on the fence and gaze at the fields of bright green grass. He was waiting for Grampa to let him out so he could run and kick up his heels and get a little exercise. "Howdy, Grampa Bill, nice day isn't it, those fields look good, all that spring grass just waitin' to be chomped up. I'm tired of this old hay. Need a change of diet." Grampa let him out of the corral and, Wow! Did that Howard run! All the way down to the pond. Farmer Brown was sitting on the pier fishing, he usually shared the catfish he caught with his buddy, Grampa Bill. "Hi Farmer Brown" said Howard, looks like they're bitin' pretty good." "Yep, they're really hitting those big, juicy worms that Grampa raises, he will be very happy with his share of catfish."

Howard trotted over to the center road and started back to his field when he heard a "Caw, Caw". He recognized Carlton the crows call, just then "plunk", Carlton landed on his shoulder. Carlton said, "It's a miracle how God changes snow and ice to a wonderful sea of bright green grass." "Howard, aren't you glad it's spring?" "This is my season," Howard said.

Meantime, way back by the machine shed where Grampa stored his tractor and other implements, that pesky Wayne and his woodchuck family were diggin' more holes in the shed floor. They dug right through that tough gravel. If they didn't quit pretty soon that old tractor would fall right in!

I heard Grampa say he was gonna trap them and take them to the big creek miles away let them dig all they want there!

When Wayne, the oldest woodchuck heard by the grapevine that he and his family were going to be sent away to the big creek they were really scared. Wayne said, "let's go to Grampa and tell him we will fill in all the holes if he lets us stay!" "Maybe he will let us dig holes under that old cabin in the woods and live with Chippy the chipmunk and his family, there's lots of room there."

The next morning, when Grampa went out to his picnic table to sit, drink his coffee and read his paper, guess what? Seven wood chucks were sitting on his picnic table! "Hi Grampa Bill," Wayne, said. (He was the oldest woodchuck.) He outlined the plan they had decided on and waited for Grampa Bill's answer. "Sounds great to me and I bless you all for coming to me with your decision, maybe I won't lose my tractor down one of your holes now!" "Great idea, Chucks."

They all strolled away, happy that everything had worked out just fine. Grampa went down the path to visit the chickens and to harvest those big, brown eggs. "Hi! Girls." He always called them girls because hens are girl chickens. Bertha and Gladys were very busy, they were cleaning out the grasshoppers from the pasture, "they're eating up all our greens!" They surely kept a clean field. Grampa leaned up against the hitching rail, took a big look around and said, "Thank you, God, for our beautiful green country!" I think I'll get a cup of coffee and sit under my maple tree on my new picnic table and just enjoy this beautiful day." "I really enjoy my farm and all my animals. God surely made a wonderful world of animals."

The Ducks and Dirty Dan

On Grampa Bill's farm there was a very large pond. This was where Danny and Doris Duck lived. The pond was very pretty, with many shrubs with berries of many colors. The duck family loved the berries, especially the red ones. Just recently, the duck family had new baby duck arrivals, ten tiny little balls of fluffy yellow feathers that almost looked like fur. In just a few days they were swimming in the pond.

Grampa's chickens, Bertha and Roger went down the road to see the new babies. "Hi, Danny and Doris, you surely have a nice family," Roger said. "You're new on the farm so you probably don't know there's a giant snappin' turtle in the far north corner of the pond and he will eat anything that gets near him!" Grampa Bill saw him a couple times and he's a monster, just about as big as a dish pan, you'd better be careful of your baby ducks!

Just as they were talking, up popped the huge head of "Dirty Dan," only about a foot away from a baby ducky. Bertha and Roger jumped up and began flying over the monster turtle, all the while cackling and chattering and putting up such a fuss that woke up Carlton the Crow that lived in the cherry tree near the pond. As he flew to the pond, he said, " Oh , Oh, it looks like Bertha and Roger need help." He dive- bombed Dirty Dan and just about hit that nasty old turtle in the head! That really scared "Old Dirty Dan" and he ducked his head under the water and swam away!

What a scare! Doris Duck was so thankful, that she hugged Bertha, Roger and Carton and promised to keep her baby ducks on the good side of the pond where it was very shallow and she could easily see the monster turtle if he came near. She said, "Thanks buddies, it's nice to know we have such good friends and that you can help keep watch on our babies."

Bertha and Roger strolled back to their field feeling like they were three feet tall heroes while Carlton flew happy circles above them.

When Grampa Bill heard about the scare and Bertha, Roger and Carlton being heroes he put out a big bowl of cracked corn and grain for all the chickens and birds in the barnyard as a super reward. This was a very special day for all! Grampa Bill said, "One day I'll catch that Dirty Dan and drive over to the reservoir and give him a new home, then my pond will be safer.

Fast Food Chickens

Grampa Bill was sitting by the barn under the big maple tree where he usually had his morning coffee, watching his chickens pecking on grass, chasing bugs and butterflies and having a good time in the yard. They liked to run in and out of the barn where Howard the horse lived and keep him company. Grampa Bill watched the chickens and thought it quite strange when most of them went over to the barn and jumped up on the hitching rail. They were staring at Grampa and kind of looking mean. His rooster "Roger" and his chicken in charge "Bertha" walked over to him and said, "Grampa Bill, we've got a complaint, we all decided we're tired of the same old chicken feed and we want something new." Grampa told them that's the only thing chickens eat, there isn't anything else. Bertha said, "Oh yes there is!" Grampa said, "what is it?" Roger and Bertha both said, "We want BIGGIE BURGERS and CURLEY FRENCH FRIES!" Grampa said," chickens don't eat Biggie burgers and French fries!" "Oh yes they do, said Roger the rooster, Farmer Brown down the road feeds his chickens Biggie Burgers and Curley French Fries…his chickens told us this." (Grampa didn't believe them!) But, he said he would go over to see Farmer Brown. Grampa Bill climbed up on his tractor and drove to Farmer Browns farm down the road to ask him if it was true.

"Hi, Farmer Brown, Hi Grampa Bill." "Farmer Brown, my chickens say you feed your chickens Biggie Burgers and Curley French Fries, is this true?" He said, "Yes!" One day he went into the house for a cup of coffee. When he came out his chickens were on the table eating his food and really enjoying it! They told him they really liked it so now he gives them burgers and fries every Saturday as a treat. He said his chickens are even laying more eggs! "Grampa Bill, I guess my chickens told your chickens how good the treat really was!" Grampa Bill went back to his chickens and told them he would do the same as what Farmer Brown did. He would give them a treat every Saturday. His chickens all ringed around him, clucking and cackling and they all looked like they were smiling! They promised him twice as many eggs! Roger the rooster and Bertha his big hen were strutting around cackling and crowing about how they talked Grampa Bill into their new treat of BIGGIE BURGERS and CURLEY FRENCH FRIES! They all went back to the barnyard and chased the bugs and butterflies and really looked happy! Well, Saturday morning came and Grampa Bill went to the Fast Food Place and bought Biggie Burgers and Curley French Fries for all his chickens. They sat on the picnic table and ate every bit! They all said, "Thanks Grampa, we will try hard to give you many more eggs." The next morning Grampa went out to the chicken coop to collect the eggs and was overjoyed at all the eggs the chickens had laid, he was getting so many eggs he brought dozens to church the next Sunday. He gave his neighbors some and said, "Call me if you need more!" Grampa was so happy, he told the chickens he would give them a ride in his new trailer on Sunday after he got home from church as a reward. They were very happy hearing that!

The next Sunday, when Grampa Bill and Gramma Sue got home from church, all ten of his chickens were sitting in his trailer, ready to go! Well…. they took a tour of the whole farm. As they went past Howard the horse's big barn where he lived, Howard came over to the fence and waved to us as we went by and said, "I'll take some of those burgers and fries, Roger the rooster was telling me about them, sounds much better than this dry old hay!" They went down the main road to the trail that went around the pond. Grampa waved to the ducks in the pond. "Hi Grampa, c'mon in and go swimming with us." they said. "No thanks, and you better watch out for that big ole "Dirty Dan" the snapper turtle, he's pretty mean and sneaky," said Grampa.

The chickens jumped down to say "Hi" to the ducks, looked for the turtle, (they had never seen a turtle!) But Dirty Dan was hiding. The chickens jumped back into the trailer and they all went to see Grampa's beehives, the bees buzzing around flying from flower to flower gathering honey and pollen, doing their busy work. Driving around the back field we saw a family of deer, they came over to us and showed Grampa their new baby deer Daisy, called a fawn, she was very pretty, light brown with white spots. "Have a good day they said." Grampa drove down the center road back to the barn where the chickens jumped out. They said, "Thanks for the tour, Grampa, we surely enjoyed it." They all went back to their coop, ready for bedtime and to dream about BIGGIE BURGERS and CURLY FRENCH FRIES!

The Terrible Storm

It was a bad storm, a terrible storm. Power lines down, trees uprooted, shingles stripped from rooftops, flooded fields….the weather radio said the wind roared through Grampa Bill's town at 73 miles per hour doing much damage. When the storm ended, Grampa Bill went out to survey the damage to his property. He was shocked to see so much wreckage, shingles from his house scattered all around the yard, his telephone line hung down in the road, the whole North field flooded. As he stood in the back yard he heard a lot of squawkin' and carrying on back by the chicken coop. Bertha and Roger, his prize chickens ran up to him. "Do you see that big cherry tree sticking out of our chicken coop?" It was the tree where Carlton the crow lived! Oh my! I hope he wasn't hurt! The tree had been sucked right out of the ground and dropped right on the chicken coop! Bertha said, "Grampa Bill, our house is smashed, the roof is caved in, where will we live?" "Not to worry," Grampa said, "Gramma Sue and I will fix up my work shop where I make my bird houses, there will be plenty of room for all of you chickens." Bertha and Roger wrangled all the chickens into the shop, they looked around and said, "this is terrible, where's our comfortable nests, our roosts?" Gramma Sue said, "We will fix some temporary furniture but you've got to bear with us, it will take a little time, please be patient." While they were standing there, they heard a tapping at the window. There was Carlton the crow waving to them, "I'm okay, he said, I was at my cousins during the storm." "I talked to Herman, the big hawk and he said I could bunk with him in his nest at the top of the great cottonwood tree."

Three days later the insurance company came out, gave Grampa an estimate and said they would fix everything.....they would even give us a new chicken coop! John, the insurance man said, "Draw up a plan Grampa Bill and we'll make a "Grand Hotel" for your chickens."

Well, it worked out swell, the chickens got their coop, Carlton the crow moved in with Herman the hawk and the construction crew gave Grampa and Gramma new roofs, new gutters, a new garage overhead door, fixed the workshop roof and.....look at that chicken coop, what a sight to see, it set out there like the "Grand Hotel"! We opened the door to the workshop and said, "Come on out all you chickens, see your new home!" They ran over to the new coop and all stood just looking. "This is so beautiful, Bertha said" and they all cheered.

A few days later, Farmer Brown stopped by. "Hi! Grampa Bill", "Bertha and Roger came by my farm and bragged about their new coop, I just had to see it!" "Wow!" "It certainly is beautiful, it was time for that 50 year old coop to go anyway!" "Grampa Bill, you've really had a blessing, from a terrible storm to a beautiful finish," and he drove away, very happy for his buddy, Grampa Bill.

Grampa Bill and Gramma Sue began cleaning up the workshop and found eggs in every place imaginable, on the bench, under shelves, behind the potbelly stove, in boxes, everywhere! It was like an Easter egg hunt!

Out of all the bad made by the storm, Grampa and Gramma were blessed with repairs making a lot of good looks to the old farm! All the animals ringed around and said, "Thanks God for this wonderful place you have given us!"

Matt's Robin

Coming home from school one day, our son Matt found a baby robin that had fallen out of a tree. Very tenderly, Matt picked up the baby bird. He wrapped it in his handkerchief and ran all the way home. Almost out of breath, he burst in the back door and cried, "Mom, Mom!" "Come here, look at what I found!" "What is it," Mom said? Matt opened his handkerchief and there it laid, a teeny, tiny, squirming baby robin!

"Can I keep it, huh, Mom? Mom said, "Why not, the zoo you have in your room with the turtles, snakes, frogs and spiders should give him lots of company!" "I do most of the feeding and watering now, what's one more mouth?"

Matt and his Mom found a small cardboard box, put in a soft cloth and set the box by the heat. He asked mom to feed it while he was in school. Mom said, "Of course….it will be fun seeing him grow up, you can make it a 'show and tell' school project, I guess you may call me your 'zoo keeper!" Mom called the library to find out what to feed the baby bird and they said, "Dig up earthworms!" You know, they're the big ones you find on the side walk after a big rain." Matt's mom cut the earthworms into tiny pieces and fed the baby robin six times a day with a tweezers and gave him water about ten times a day using an eye dropper. The tiny bird grew stronger and stronger each day and pretty soon he grew fuzzy little feathers, his wings got bigger and one day Matt found him standing on top of his box! Matt was so excited, he called us to his room shouting, "Look at Robby!" There that bird stood, looking pretty proud of himself! That's when we decided Robby was a good name for him!

Matt built Robby a bigger cage and pretty soon he could eat worms out of mom's hand and drink water from a bowl. One day, Matt found Robby walking around his room. Matt said," "Robby, we're going to take you outside so you can have fun walking around and see all the outside sights and we'll teach you how to drink from a bird bath and teach you how to take a bath, how to scratch worms. You'll have lots of fun, Robby. We all went out to the backyard to see Robby drink and bathe. He didn't have a Mommy so we had to teach him everything.

Each day we would take Robby outside when Matt got home from school. Robby would follow us everywhere, walking behind us making funny little noises and little chuckles like he was very happy. We would set him in the birdbath and he would drink and we'd splash water on him. He really enjoyed that. One day he flapped his wings, jumped from the birdbath and flew to the ground! We were really surprised! Matt said, "Robby finally graduated!" Robby still went with us each day, we would take him outside to the compost pile where he would jump up on a post and make chuckling noises until he was fed. Now that he knew he could fly, when we took him outside he would fly to the post by the compost pile and wait to be fed his worms!

One day, Mom put a worm down and took his foot and scratched a worm. He got the message that this was his food and scratched each worm Mom gave him and then he would eat it. Whenever he ate a worm, he would chuckle like he was happy!

It was getting late in the summer and Robby was getting bigger, his feathers were turning colors, a gray and brown top and a red breast. That's why they are called "Robin Red Breast."

One day Robby ran across the yard and suddenly took flight, flew away and out of sight. We all felt very sad and thought we would never see him again. We felt like we had lost a friend, and tears came to our eyes. One day when Dad came home from work, he got out of the car, gave us all hugs and asked if we had seen Robby? No, we said, he's been gone all day. Dad said he would try whistling for him, (He saw this on T.V. once!) He whistled three times….and….Suddenly….out of nowhere, our Robby flew to his outstretched arm. We all found out then if we whistled, he would come back to us. For quite a while Robby answered our whistle and sometimes just dropped in for a visit. Sometimes he would land on our lawn, walk around with us and fly over to the compost pile, (He was digging his own worms now!) Mom taught him well! Then…away he would fly. We always wondered where he had flown.

One Sunday we had a patio party with several guests. We told them the story of how we had raised a Robin from a rescued newly born robin that had fallen out of the nest to a self sufficient adult bird. We had home schooled him! One of the guests laughed and said, "That's preposterous!" Dad stood up and whistled a few times and guess what? Robby flew in and landed on this man's knee, we all laughed and Robby flew away. Our guest was shocked, he said, "He had never been this close to a real bird in all his life." The guests were all amazed!

Well, we saw Robby a few times after that, he flew in when Dad whistled a few times and once he walked around the lawn and then flew to the compost pile, scratched a few worms and took off. We never saw him again. We felt as if we lost a friend but we realized he needed his own life in the wild hanging around with other Robins. This was an experience we will always remember.

Now when we see a Robin on our lawn, we wonder, is it Robby?

Grampa's Raccoon

It was a beautiful fall day, not a cloud in the sky, warm and fresh, the smell of burning leaves floating in the air smelled great. Grampa Bill and Gramma Sue were raking leaves, wishing they didn't have so many trees! When ……out of the corner of his eye Grampa saw something move! All of a sudden….out of the hedgerow stepped a large raccoon……he walked toward Grampa, stopped in front of him, looked right up at Grampa's face for a minute, then turned and walked away! "What do you make of that?" Gramma Sue asked Grampa, seems kind of odd, it looked like he wanted to tell you something, haven't seen him around before." Grampa said, "He looked right into my eyes, his eyes looked kind of sorrowful."

They went on raking and talking and enjoying the day…when the same raccoon walked out of the hedges again! He walked right up to Grampa, stood up on his hind legs, put his front feet on Grampa's knees and said, "My home got drowned out when the creek flooded, I lost my home!" He said, "I saw a great big cottonwood tree down the side road with a big hole in it, I wonder if I could rent that?" Grampa said, "We surely would like you to live here but we don't charge rent, all we ask is that you get along with the other animals, I'll introduce you to all the other animals after church this Sunday." The raccoon said, "that sounds great, by the way, my name is Rocky." "I know you are Grampa Bill, the lady across the road said I should see you, she said I would really like it here, I know I'm going to like it here." "I've got to go now and pretty up my new home, I'm excited, this is the start of a new life, God is really awesome isn't He?" "See you later, Grampa and Gramma." "Thanks a lot." Rocky waved and strolled away, knowing he had found new friends and a new home.

Gramma Sue stood there, leaning on her rake, "Well, if you don't beat that!" "Rocky is certainly a gentleman." "Too bad he can't rake leaves!"

At that moment Carlton Crow flew down and landed on Grampa's rake, "It looks like you've got another tenant, Grampa." Grampa said, "Did you hear what he said?" "Nah, Carlton said, I read lips and have a great pair of eyes!" With that, Cartlton flew away to catch up with Rocky to help him find the way and to get better acquainted. "Hey, Rocky...I'll introduce you to Herman, he's a great big hawk but a real nice guy." "It's his tree but he won't mind another tenant, the tree is mighty big." "Grampa Bill says it's probably one hundred years old!"

With the leaf raking partly done, Grampa and Gramma sat down on their patio chairs, looking at the great expanse of a back yard covered with about eight inches deep of maple leaves from last fall! "What do you say we call our pastor at church and ask the Youth Group for help?" "Good idea, Bill," Gramma Sue said, "Let's go inside and make supper."

The Rental Wren

Grampa Bill had been sick and when he got home from the hospital, he was told he must rest and not do anything heavy but could work a little in his woodshop. Wally, his buddy called one day and said, he had a load of very old cedar fence panels he wanted to dispose of as his company couldn't burn them any more in his town, could he drop them off at Grampa's farm? Grampa said, "I don't know what I'll do with them but bring 'em over." The next day, here comes a truck about the size of a semi hauling a flatbed of picket fence panels! Grampa Bill said,"What am I gonna do with all this?"........Wally said, "Make birdhouses!"

Well, that's just what Grampa did! He made 20 different bird house models in his shop, mounted them on a fence panel, added wheels and each morning he would tow them with his Old Ford tractor to the road in front with a big "For Sale" sign.

One morning, before towing out the display, while eating breakfast, Grampa's son Billy looked out the window and said, "Look at the wren on the bird houses!" Grampa Bill said, "That's Willie Wren, he and his wife Wilma put up a nest in our yard every spring, sometimes they put a nest in my shop or garage!" We all went out to see which house he would pick. "Hi Willie," Grampa said, "how do you like my new bird houses?" Willie, hopping from birdhouse to birdhouse said, "I'm really impressed, I like them all, you really did a nice job, Grampa." We all watched as the tiny bird hopped from house to house, looking in, sometimes going all the way in and then he pulled one of Grampa's fluorescent price tags off and said, "This looks great, see you later Grampa Bill." And he flew away. Billy said, "He's probably going to show his wife that he found a terrific rental!"

Days went by and soon the pair of wrens came back and set up housekeeping in a very old, rustic wren birdhouse way up on a post, nowhere near all the other new birdhouses!"

Willie told Grampa that Wilma liked the 'homespun' look, it felt kinda homey! Well, soon we were treated to a delightful experience seeing the activity of nest building, egg laying and the tiny peeps as mom and dad wren flew in with morsels of food for the hungry babies. We left for a week end and didn't get to see the fledglings but the experience was priceless. We can't wait 'til we meet some of Willie's family flying around.

Buddy & Peaches

Sometime ago, Grampa Bill found a baby kitty and almost the same time his son Billy found a stray puppy. Billy named him Buddy and Grampa named his kitty Peaches. Peaches grew up and one day she told Grampa how happy she was at her new home. She loved the farm and being able to talk to all the friendly animals. Sometimes Billy would bring Buddy to the farm and he and Peaches would play together for hours, wrestling, running up and down the trails chasing each other. Buddy would pretend to bite her and Peaches would smack him on the nose with her paw. It was good fun. It looked like they were fighting but they would never hurt each other, they were the best of friends. Buddy told Grampa he would always take care of Peaches and watch over her.

Each night Grampa Bill would put Peaches to bed in the garage as he was afraid that Sneaky Sam the Coyote that lived on the farm might harm her, each night she would thank Grampa for taking such good care of her. She liked sleeping on the tractor seat. Gramma Sue had put a big fluffy pillow there for her. In the morning when she saw Grampa come in the door she would say, "Morning Gramps" and jump over to the workbench where her food bowl was and wait for her favorite kitty food.

One morning Grampa opened up the garage and Peaches was gone! She was nowhere in sight! Calling and calling and whistling for her but no answer. She was gone! That's when Grampa saw he had forgotten to close the side window! He ran outside and looked around the Garage but…….no Peaches! Running into the house Grampa called Billy on the phone, "Billy, come over here with Buddy, Peaches is gone and maybe Buddy can find her!" When Billy and Buddy arrived Buddy sat down while Grampa told him about Peaches getting lost. Buddy said, "I'll run down all the paths and roads and bark while I'm running, Peaches will recognize my bark and will meow real loud." Billy drove down to Farmer Browns to see if she might be there, she liked to visit with Farmer Brown. "Nope, she hasn't been here," Farmer Brown said.

Billy knew Buddy would hear her meow. He prayed he could find her and began running down the center road, calling and whistling for her. Grampa walked down the side road doing the same. All of a sudden Billy heard Buddy barking. Billy ran as fast as he could through the bushes and trees, running to the sound of Buddy barking, "She's here, she's here! Billy almost ran into Grampa racing down the road! There was Peaches, sitting at the top of the shed crying and meowing with tears running down her cheeks because she couldn't get down.

Billy ran and got a big ladder, climbed up and Peaches jumped onto his shoulder, she licked his face and said, "I was really scared Billy, I jumped out of the garage window and decided to take a moonlight stroll when I ran onto that terrible sneaky coyote, he chased me and I climbed that big tree by the shed, jumped to the roof and he couldn't get me, he ran off when he heard people coming. I promise I'll never go out at night again.

When Billy put her on the ground, she and Buddy danced and danced, around and around, wrestling with each other. Buddy kissed her nose, he was so happy! Grampa grabbed them both, hugged them and kissed them. Back at the house they each got a can of tuna and they sat and ate together. Billy put Buddy in his truck, Peaches and Grampa said thank you and waved as they drove off. Grampa put Peaches in the garage, closed the window, picked her up, hugged her and put her on the tractor seat with that big fluffy pillow. He heard her say, "Meow, meow." It sounded like, "Thank you, thank you. Grampa hugged her and kissed her again and then, she fell asleep!

Printed in the United States
By Bookmasters